THE ——— GARDEN
PLANNER AND RECORD BOOK
Caroline Ash

Produced for
National Home Gardening Club
12301 Whitewater Drive
Minnetonka, Minnesota

Vice President, Product Marketing Mike Vail
Vice President, Product Marketing Cal Franklin
Book Products Development Director Tom Carpenter
Design Bernard Higton
Text Caroline Ash
Managing Editor Jemima Dunne
Managing Art Editor Philip Gilderdale
Senior Art Editor Karen Ward
Project Editor Annelise Evans
Production Maryann Rogers
US Editors Laaren Brown, Ray Rogers

Special photography Guy Ryecart, Clive Streeter, Meg Sullivan
Border illustration Jane Thomson

First American Edition, 1997
2 4 6 8 10 9 7 5 3 1

Published in the United States by
DK Publishing, Inc.
95 Madison Avenue, New York, New York 10016
Visit us on the World Wide Web at http://www.dk.com

Copyright © 1997
Dorling Kindersley Limited, London

ISBN 0-7894-1472-4

Color reproduction in Italy by Editrice, Verona
Printed and bound in Singapore by Tien Wah Press Pte Ltd.

CONTENTS

Introduction 4

INTRODUCTION

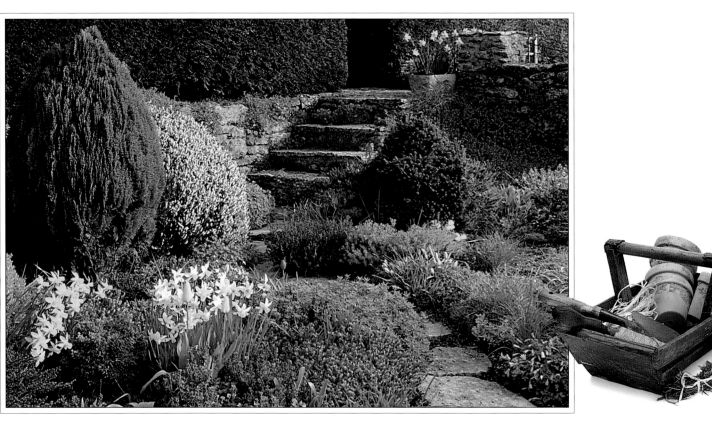

Creating a beautiful garden is a considerable achievement, demanding both horticultural and design skills. The different elements must mesh successfully to produce an integrated and pleasing result. A well-planned garden should be in proportion and harmony with its surroundings and should complement the nearby buildings.

A garden can always be refined or altered. This book enables you to write down new ideas as they occur to you, make lists of any new plants you would like to grow, and jot down reminders about plants that need your attention. You can list plants you would like to plant more of, and make a note of planting combinations that particularly appeal to you. Keeping a diary that shows how your garden develops, and a notebook of what happens each month, can be invaluable in helping you create the perfect yet everchanging effect. It can also be great fun. Gardening is truly a pleasure that grows over time.

GARDEN DESCRIPTION

SIZE OF GARDEN

....

TYPE OF SOIL

....

LOCAL CLIMATE

....

EXPOSURE

....

DESCRIPTION OF BOUNDARIES

....

STRONG FEATURES

....

WEAK FEATURES

....

AREAS FOR IMPROVEMENT

PHOTOGRAPH OF YOUR GARDEN

I hold that the best purpose of a
garden is to give delight and to give
refreshment of mind, to soothe, to refine,
and to lift up the heart.

GERTRUDE JEKYLL

PART ONE

CREATING YOUR GARDEN

This section will help you plan your garden,
keep detailed notes on its planting and development,
and record all your gardening activities.

FAVORITE PLANTS

When deciding on suitable plants for your garden, you are likely to begin by choosing plants that are your favorites for a variety of reasons – because they are visually appealing, because they complement the other plants, or because you feel they are essential to have in a garden. However, when choosing potential plants, it is also worth considering other factors: the flowers; the type and color of foliage; the potential height, spread, and shape of the plant; and its season of interest. Take into account the type of soil you have, and its condition, and the amount of sun or shade different parts of your garden offer. All this information will enable you to choose plants to flower or provide interest for as long a period as possible. In the fall and winter, when few plants produce flowers, make a note of those that produce spectacular foliage, berries, or fruits.

PERENNIALS

NAME	NAME	NAME	NAME
SIZE AND SHAPE	SIZE AND SHAPE	SIZE AND SHAPE	SIZE AND SHAPE
KEY FEATURE	KEY FEATURE	KEY FEATURE	KEY FEATURE
BEST SEASON	BEST SEASON	BEST SEASON	BEST SEASON
PLANT NEEDS	PLANT NEEDS	PLANT NEEDS	PLANT NEEDS

NAME	NAME	NAME	NAME
SIZE AND SHAPE	SIZE AND SHAPE	SIZE AND SHAPE	SIZE AND SHAPE
KEY FEATURE	KEY FEATURE	KEY FEATURE	KEY FEATURE
BEST SEASON	BEST SEASON	BEST SEASON	BEST SEASON
PLANT NEEDS	PLANT NEEDS	PLANT NEEDS	PLANT NEEDS

NAME	NAME	NAME
SIZE AND SHAPE	SIZE AND SHAPE	SIZE AND SHAPE
KEY FEATURE	KEY FEATURE	KEY FEATURE
BEST SEASON	BEST SEASON	BEST SEASON
PLANT NEEDS	PLANT NEEDS	PLANT NEEDS

ANNUALS AND BIENNIALS

BULBS

NAME
....

SIZE AND SHAPE
....

KEY FEATURE
....

BEST SEASON
....

PLANT NEEDS

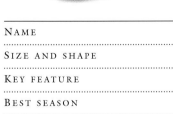

NAME
....

SIZE AND SHAPE
....

KEY FEATURE
....

BEST SEASON
....

PLANT NEEDS

NAME
....

SIZE AND SHAPE
....

KEY FEATURE
....

BEST SEASON
....

PLANT NEEDS

NAME
....

SIZE AND SHAPE
....

KEY FEATURE
....

BEST SEASON
....

PLANT NEEDS

NAME
....

SIZE AND SHAPE
....

KEY FEATURE
....

BEST SEASON
....

PLANT NEEDS

NAME
....

SIZE AND SHAPE
....

KEY FEATURE
....

BEST SEASON
....

PLANT NEEDS

NAME
....

SIZE AND SHAPE
....

KEY FEATURE
....

BEST SEASON
....

PLANT NEEDS

NAME
....

SIZE AND SHAPE
....

KEY FEATURE
....

BEST SEASON
....

PLANT NEEDS

NAME
....

SIZE AND SHAPE
....

KEY FEATURE
....

BEST SEASON
....

PLANT NEEDS

NAME
....

SIZE AND SHAPE
....

KEY FEATURE
....

BEST SEASON
....

PLANT NEEDS

NAME
....

SIZE AND SHAPE
....

KEY FEATURE
....

BEST SEASON
....

PLANT NEEDS

TREES AND SHRUBS

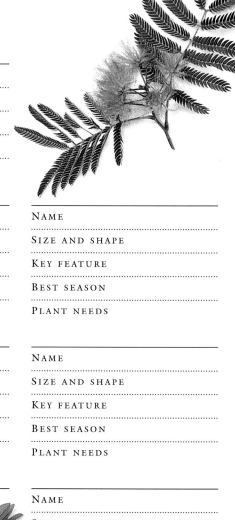

NAME
....
SIZE AND SHAPE
....
KEY FEATURE
....
BEST SEASON
....
PLANT NEEDS
....

NAME
....
SIZE AND SHAPE
....
KEY FEATURE
....
BEST SEASON
....
PLANT NEEDS
....

NAME
....
SIZE AND SHAPE
....
KEY FEATURE
....
BEST SEASON
....
PLANT NEEDS
....

NAME
....
SIZE AND SHAPE
....
KEY FEATURE
....
BEST SEASON
....
PLANT NEEDS
....

NAME
....
SIZE AND SHAPE
....
KEY FEATURE
....
BEST SEASON
....
PLANT NEEDS
....

NAME
....
SIZE AND SHAPE
....
KEY FEATURE
....
BEST SEASON
....
PLANT NEEDS
....

NAME
....
SIZE AND SHAPE
....
KEY FEATURE
....
BEST SEASON
....
PLANT NEEDS
....

NAME
....
SIZE AND SHAPE
....
KEY FEATURE
....
BEST SEASON
....
PLANT NEEDS
....

NAME
....
SIZE AND SHAPE
....
KEY FEATURE
....
BEST SEASON
....
PLANT NEEDS
....

NAME
....
SIZE AND SHAPE
....
KEY FEATURE
....
BEST SEASON
....
PLANT NEEDS
....

NAME
....
SIZE AND SHAPE
....
KEY FEATURE
....
BEST SEASON
....
PLANT NEEDS
....

NAME
....
SIZE AND SHAPE
....
KEY FEATURE
....
BEST SEASON
....
PLANT NEEDS
....

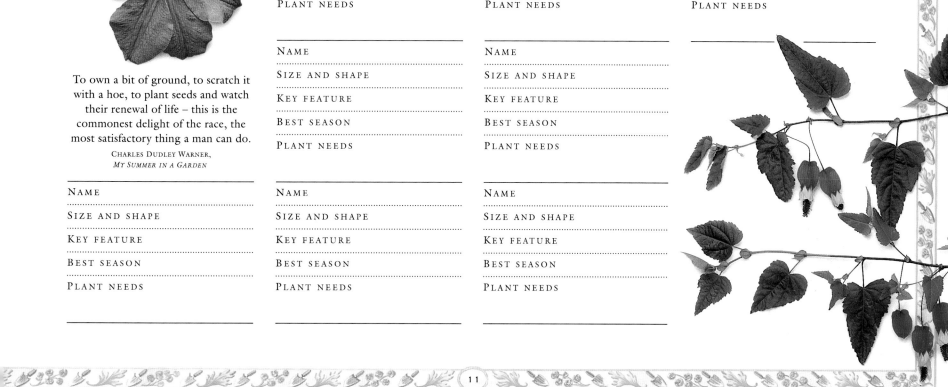

CLIMBERS

NAME
....
SIZE AND SHAPE
....
KEY FEATURE
....
BEST SEASON
....
PLANT NEEDS

NAME
....
SIZE AND SHAPE
....
KEY FEATURE
....
BEST SEASON
....
PLANT NEEDS

NAME
....
SIZE AND SHAPE
....
KEY FEATURE
....
BEST SEASON
....
PLANT NEEDS

NAME
....
SIZE AND SHAPE
....
KEY FEATURE
....
BEST SEASON
....
PLANT NEEDS

NAME
....
SIZE AND SHAPE
....
KEY FEATURE
....
BEST SEASON
....
PLANT NEEDS

NAME
....
SIZE AND SHAPE
....
KEY FEATURE
....
BEST SEASON
....
PLANT NEEDS

NAME
....
SIZE AND SHAPE
....
KEY FEATURE
....
BEST SEASON
....
PLANT NEEDS

NAME
....
SIZE AND SHAPE
....
KEY FEATURE
....
BEST SEASON
....
PLANT NEEDS

NAME
....
SIZE AND SHAPE
....
KEY FEATURE
....
BEST SEASON
....
PLANT NEEDS

To own a bit of ground, to scratch it with a hoe, to plant seeds and watch their renewal of life – this is the commonest delight of the race, the most satisfactory thing a man can do.

CHARLES DUDLEY WARNER,
MY SUMMER IN A GARDEN

NAME
....
SIZE AND SHAPE
....
KEY FEATURE
....
BEST SEASON
....
PLANT NEEDS

NAME
....
SIZE AND SHAPE
....
KEY FEATURE
....
BEST SEASON
....
PLANT NEEDS

NAME
....
SIZE AND SHAPE
....
KEY FEATURE
....
BEST SEASON
....
PLANT NEEDS

GARDEN PLANS

These grids can be used to draw a scaled-down plan of your garden and record the position of existing plants, or to plan future planting areas. Plants may be numbered on each grid and the plant names entered beside the corresponding number in the key accompanying the grid. No garden ever remains the same for any length of time, and you will probably want to alter these plans to incorporate new planting, and changes to your garden, as it develops and matures. Alternatively, photocopy these pages so that you can refine your plans as your garden changes over the years.

KEY TO AREA ONE

1 ....

2 ....

3 ....

4 ....

5 ....

6 ....

7 ....

8 ....

9 ....

10 ....

11 ....

12 ....

13 ....

14 ....

15 ....

16 ....

17 ....

18 ....

19 ....

20 ....

21 ....

22 ....

23 ....

24 ....

25 ....

26 ....

27 ....

28 ....

29 ....

30 ....

The story of mankind began in a garden and ended in revelations.

OSCAR WILDE
A WOMAN OF NO IMPORTANCE

AREA ONE

AREA TWO

KEY TO AREA TWO

1
2
3
4
5
6
7
8
9
10
11
12

The country habit has me by the heart,
For he's bewitched for ever who has seen,
Not with his eyes but with his vision, Spring
Flow down the woods and stipple leaves with sun.

VITA SACKVILLE-WEST, *THE LAND, WINTER*

13
14
15
16
17
18
19
20
21
22

AREA THREE

KEY TO AREA THREE

1 ....
2 ....
3 ....
4 ....
5 ....
6 ....
7 ....
8 ....

9 ....
10 ....
11 ....
12 ....
13 ....
14 ....
15 ....
16 ....

17 ....
18 ....
19 ....
20 ....
21 ....
22 ....
23 ....
24 ....

PLANTING RECORDS

Keeping a record of any new plants you acquire is extremely useful. If you wish to purchase a similar plant in the future, you can use these notes to look up the name and description of the plant and the supplier. This record also serves as a reminder in years to come, when the plant label has faded or disappeared from the garden. Planting a tree or long-lived shrub or climber gives a structure to the garden and is an investment in posterity. Keeping a record of these plants will be of interest to you or future owners of your garden in the years ahead.

PERENNIALS

NAME	WHERE PURCHASED	WHERE PLANTED	DATE

ANNUALS AND BIENNIALS

NAME	WHERE PURCHASED	WHERE PLANTED	DATE

BULBS

NAME	WHERE PURCHASED	WHERE PLANTED	DATE

SHRUBS

NAME	WHERE PURCHASED	WHERE PLANTED	DATE

A plant is like a self-willed man, out of whom we can obtain all
which we desire, if we will only treat him his own way.

JOHANN WOLFGANG VON GOETHE, *ELECTIVE AFFINITIES*

CLIMBERS

NAME	WHERE PURCHASED	WHERE PLANTED	DATE

TREES

NAME	WHERE PURCHASED	WHERE PLANTED	DATE

PROPAGATION

Increasing your stock of plants by propagation is both economical and rewarding as long as you follow the basic guidelines and choose a suitable technique. There are four principal methods: you can raise plants from seed, or from cuttings; or through division; or layering. Growing plants from seed is very satisfying, although some seed is difficult or slow to germinate. It is the easiest method of raising a large number of plants, and is the best means of propagation for many herbaceous plants. Taking cuttings is the most widespread vegetative practice, although it does demand a degree of skill. Once mastered, it is a reliable means of propagating a plant with the same characteristics as its parent. Division is the simplest method, and many clump-forming perennials and bulbs benefit from dividing. Layering is commonly used for trees, shrubs, and climbers, as growing these plants from seed can be an extremely slow process.

RECORD OF SEEDS SOWN

NAME	DATE SOWN	DATE GERMINATED	DATE TRANSPLANTED	COMMENTS

In seed time learn, in harvest teach, in winter enjoy.
WILLIAM BLAKE, *THE MARRIAGE OF HEAVEN AND HELL*

RECORD OF CUTTINGS

PARENT PLANT	DATE TAKEN	DATE ROOTED	COMMENTS

RECORD OF DIVISION

PARENT PLANT	DATE DIVIDED	DATE PLANTED OUT	COMMENTS

RECORD OF LAYERING

PARENT PLANT	DATE TAKEN	DATE LAYERED	COMMENTS

VEGETABLES

Cultivating your own food satisfies a basic instinct, and has many advantages. Little can match the flavor of freshly picked, home-grown vegetables, and varieties that are unusual or difficult to obtain can be grown in abundance and without the use of chemicals. Growing your own food also saves money. A gardener can feel proud of being able to feed his friends and family with produce harvested from the garden. If space is at a premium, vegetables can be grown successfully in a wide variety of containers or can be incorporated in a mixed border. Many can be grown vertically, instead of only at ground level, and will grow happily up tepees of stakes or other frames. Choose compact and fast-growing varieties and plant a small amount of each crop. By successive planting of seasonal crops it is possible to maximize the harvest reaped in a confined space.

RECORD OF VEGETABLES GROWN

NAME

DATE PLANTED   DATE HARVESTED

COMMENTS ON CROP

NAME

DATE PLANTED   DATE HARVESTED

COMMENTS ON CROP

What a man needs in gardening is a cast-iron
back, with a hinge in it.
CHARLES DUDLEY WARNER, *MY SUMMER IN A GARDEN*

NAME

DATE PLANTED   DATE HARVESTED

COMMENTS ON CROP

NAME

DATE PLANTED   DATE HARVESTED

COMMENTS ON CROP

NAME

DATE PLANTED   DATE HARVESTED

COMMENTS ON CROP

NAME

DATE PLANTED   DATE HARVESTED

COMMENTS ON CROP

NAME
....

DATE PLANTED   DATE HARVESTED
....

COMMENTS ON CROP
....

NAME
....

DATE PLANTED   DATE HARVESTED
....

COMMENTS ON CROP
....

NAME
....

DATE PLANTED   DATE HARVESTED
....

COMMENTS ON CROP
....

NAME
....

DATE PLANTED   DATE HARVESTED
....

COMMENTS ON CROP
....

CHECKLIST OF TASKS

Spring
Plant out perennial vegetables; start planting out annual vegetables, under cover if necessary; mulch in late spring; water thoroughly; sow seed of tender vegetables indoors, and seed of hardy vegetables outdoors.

Summer
Plant out winter brassicas, salad vegetables and tender vegetables; water as necessary; train climbing vegetables; harvest and store produce; sow seed of summer crops; begin sowing seed of winter vegetables.

Fall
Plant out winter salad vegetables under cover; start preparing empty beds; harvest and store produce; protect tender crops and perennials; sow seed of salad crops under cover.

Winter
Finish preparing empty beds; prepare seedbeds; stake and protect vegetables as necessary; sow seed indoors.

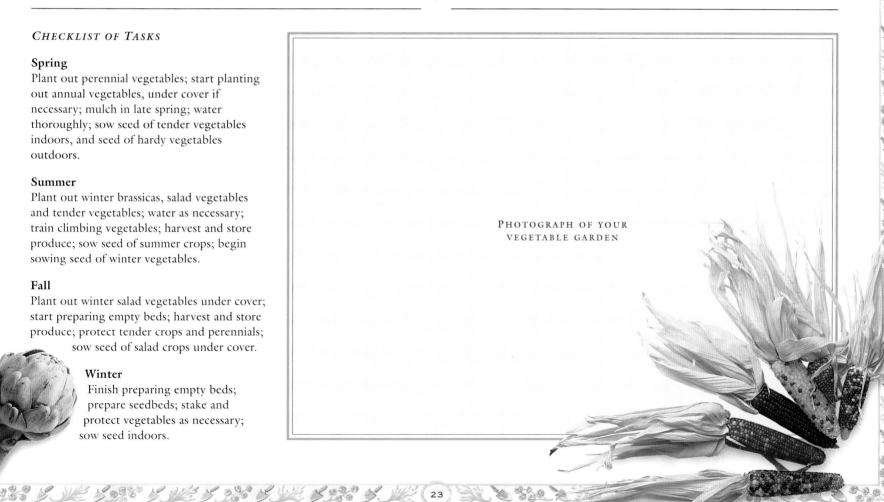

PHOTOGRAPH OF YOUR
VEGETABLE GARDEN

FRUIT

While growing vegetables frequently requires intensive labor, fruit trees and bushes usually need less attention. However, many fruit trees require pruning, thinning, and spraying, and bushes need to be tied in. If possible, choose disease-resistant, long-lived varieties. A fruit tree can form a focal point among herbaceous perennials, contributing glorious blossoms in the spring, and colorful foliage and fruits later in the year. Fruit bushes can be planted in a mixed border, as long as there is easy access for picking. Many dwarf varieties of fruit trees have been bred to grow and flourish in containers.

RECORD OF FRUIT TREES GROWN

NAME

DATE PLANTED   DATE HARVESTED

COMMENTS ON CROP

NAME

DATE PLANTED   DATE HARVESTED

COMMENTS ON CROP

NAME

DATE PLANTED   DATE HARVESTED

COMMENTS ON CROP

NAME

DATE PLANTED

DATE HARVESTED

COMMENTS ON CROP

NAME

DATE PLANTED   DATE HARVESTED

COMMENTS ON CROP

NAME

DATE PLANTED   DATE HARVESTED

COMMENTS ON CROP

NAME

DATE PLANTED   DATE HARVESTED

COMMENTS ON CROP

NAME

DATE PLANTED

DATE HARVESTED

COMMENTS ON CROP

PLANTS NEEDING SPECIAL ATTENTION

NAME

SPECIAL NEEDS

NAME

SPECIAL NEEDS

NAME

SPECIAL NEEDS

CHECKLIST OF TASKS

Spring
Begin to feed, mulch, and water fruits; check nets, stakes, and ties; pollinate as necessary; prune stone-fruit trees and trained trees; bark-ring apple and pear trees as necessary.

Summer
Replenish mulch and give liquid feed; water as required; thin out tree fruits if needed; pinch out and train shoots of fan-trained trees; prune summer-fruiting raspberries; summer-prune trained apples, pears, and plums; take leaf-bud cuttings of blackberries.

Fall
Plant tree, bush, and cane fruits; transplant fruit trees; harvest fruits, burn debris and store produce; check stakes and ties; remove old canes and tie in new ones; plant runners and sow seed of strawberries; winter-prune apples, pears, and fruit bushes; divide rooted suckers of raspberries.

Winter
Plant tree, bush, and cane fruits; protect tender outdoor fruits; repot or top-dress container-grown fruits; prune blackcurrants and blackberries.

According to ancient beliefs and customs:

Hanging mothballs around a fruit tree is a cure for leaf curl.

It is mutually beneficial to plant strawberries near beans and lettuces.

If the sun shines through apple trees on Christmas Eve or Easter Day, the next crop will be prolific, and their owner will have a good year.

It is unlucky to gather blackberries after St. Michaelmas' day (September 29).

RECORD OF SOFT FRUIT GROWN

NAME

DATE PLANTED   DATE HARVESTED

COMMENTS ON CROP

NAME

DATE PLANTED   DATE HARVESTED

COMMENTS ON CROP

NAME

DATE PLANTED   DATE HARVESTED

COMMENTS ON CROP

NAME

DATE PLANTED   DATE HARVESTED

COMMENTS ON CROP

NAME

DATE PLANTED   DATE HARVESTED

COMMENTS ON CROP

NAME

DATE PLANTED   DATE HARVESTED

COMMENTS ON CROP

THE HERB GARDEN

Herbs need to be readily accessible if they are to be picked and used, so it is best to position them near the kitchen door. They can be grown among other plants, in pots, or in a herb garden. Many herbs originate from the Mediterranean; these flourish in poor soil in a bright, sunny spot. Growing your own guarantees an abundant supply. Gather fresh herbs at their peak and use them immediately, or dry them for use throughout the year. Frequent cutting and trimming of herbs prompts new growth and means you can pick your herbs as you need them. Most herbs require little maintenance, apart from an annual cut-back and trimming. Foliage removed when pruning can be used in the kitchen as needed. Herbs are valued for many reasons, and are grown not only for their culinary uses, but for medicinal and cosmetic purposes.

RECORD OF HERBS GROWN

NAME	DATE PLANTED
USES	

NAME	DATE PLANTED
USES	

NAME	DATE PLANTED
USES	

NAME	DATE PLANTED
USES	

NAME	DATE PLANTED
USES	

NAME	DATE PLANTED
USES	

NAME	DATE PLANTED
USES	

NAME	DATE PLANTED
USES	

NAME	DATE PLANTED
USES	

NAME	DATE PLANTED
USES	

NAME	DATE PLANTED
USES	

Speak not – whisper not;
Here bloweth thyme and bergamot;
Softly on the evening hour,
Secret herbs their spices shower.

WALTER DE LA MARE,
THE SUNKEN GARDEN

ROCK PLANTS

Rock-garden plants originate in alpine conditions and thrive on what appears to be inhospitable terrain, on rocky, thin soils. Well-drained rock or gravel gardens provide ideal conditions, as most rock-garden plants grow best in an open, sunny place, although some prefer the shade provided by rocks. Many are ideal for growing in cracks and crevices. The majority of rock-garden plants are small and compact to reduce their wind resistance, and are able to withstand extreme weather conditions, from heavy snow to brilliant sunshine. Their compact growing habit and tough, leathery, or hairy leaves help conserve moisture, making them drought-tolerant. The key to success with rock-garden plants is to keep them from becoming too wet in winter, as they will rot. Once established, most plants require minimal maintenance and will continue to flower happily for years.

RECORD OF ROCK GARDEN PLANTS GROWN

NAME

WHEN IN FLOWER   DATE PLANTED

NAME

WHEN IN FLOWER   DATE PLANTED

NAME

WHEN IN FLOWER   DATE PLANTED

NAME

WHEN IN FLOWER   DATE PLANTED

NAME

WHEN IN FLOWER   DATE PLANTED

NAME

WHEN IN FLOWER   DATE PLANTED

NAME

WHEN IN FLOWER   DATE PLANTED

NAME

WHEN IN FLOWER   DATE PLANTED

NAME

WHEN IN FLOWER   DATE PLANTED

NAME

WHEN IN FLOWER   DATE PLANTED

NAME

WHEN IN FLOWER   DATE PLANTED

NAME

WHEN IN FLOWER   DATE PLANTED

NAME

WHEN IN FLOWER   DATE PLANTED

NAME

WHEN IN FLOWER   DATE PLANTED

A rock garden cannot be bought outright, like a diamond necklace, and kept without further trouble. It is nothing unless its owner loves it and understands it.

ARTHUR CLUTTON-BROCK, *THE TIMES*

CONTAINERS

Almost any container looks attractive in the garden; old stone sinks and wooden barrels are classic favorites. Terra-cotta or glazed pots are readily available, while copper, lead, and stone containers add a unique touch. Containers are also useful for growing plants that can be used to fill in gaps in borders. The only requirements are that the container must have drainage holes in the bottom and should be able to withstand wind, rain, and frost. Some pots do not even need the addition of plants to look beautiful – think of them as pieces of sculpture.

Plain pots can provide a peaceful contrast to colorful planting; by the same token, brightly colored containers will enliven a quiet corner of the garden. Window boxes and hanging baskets are an attractive way to grow plants at different heights, rather than restricting everything to ground level.

POTS

DESCRIPTION

DATE PLANTED

SEASON OF INTEREST

PLANTS

DESCRIPTION

DATE PLANTED

SEASON OF INTEREST

PLANTS

DESCRIPTION

DATE PLANTED

SEASON OF INTEREST

PLANTS

DESCRIPTION

DATE PLANTED

SEASON OF INTEREST

PLANTS

HANGING BASKETS

DESCRIPTION
....

DATE PLANTED
....

SEASON OF
INTEREST
....

PLANTS

DESCRIPTION

DATE PLANTED
....

SEASON OF INTEREST
....

PLANTS

DESCRIPTION

DATE PLANTED
....

SEASON OF INTEREST
....

PLANTS

DESCRIPTION

DATE PLANTED
....

SEASON OF INTEREST
....

PLANTS

WINDOW BOXES

DESCRIPTION
....

DATE PLANTED
....

SEASON OF INTEREST
....

PLANTS

DESCRIPTION

DATE PLANTED
....

SEASON OF INTEREST
....

PLANTS

DESCRIPTION

DATE PLANTED
....

SEASON OF INTEREST
....

PLANTS

DESCRIPTION

DATE PLANTED
....

SEASON OF INTEREST
....

PLANTS

THE WATER GARDEN

Water adds a new dimension to the garden. Flowing water, such as a garden stream or a fountain, makes a soothing, refreshing, repetitive sound, while still water is tranquil and calming. Water draws the eye, accentuates the shape of plants by adding reflections, and gives off shimmering patterns of light. The lush green foliage of many moisture-loving plants grown around the side of a pond contrasts with those in drier parts of the garden and increases the range of plants that can be grown.

Oxygenating plants help keep the pond water clear and enable you to create your own micro-ecoclimate. Water and plants work together to create an environment attractive to wildlife. If you keep a few fish, they will keep the mosquito population down and fill the pond with color and movement.

RECORD OF WATER-GARDEN PLANTS

NAME	DATE PLANTED
DEPTH PLANTED	WHEN IN FLOWER
COMMENTS	

NAME	DATE PLANTED
DEPTH PLANTED	WHEN IN FLOWER
COMMENTS	

NAME	DATE PLANTED
DEPTH PLANTED	WHEN IN FLOWER
COMMENTS	

NAME	DATE PLANTED
DEPTH PLANTED	WHEN IN FLOWER
COMMENTS	

NAME	
DATE PLANTED	
DEPTH PLANTED	
WHEN IN FLOWER	
COMMENTS	

NAME	DATE PLANTED
DEPTH PLANTED	WHEN IN FLOWER
COMMENTS	

NAME	DATE PLANTED
DEPTH PLANTED	WHEN IN FLOWER
COMMENTS	

NAME	DATE PLANTED
DEPTH PLANTED	WHEN IN FLOWER
COMMENTS	

NAME	DATE PLANTED
DEPTH PLANTED	WHEN IN FLOWER
COMMENTS	

NAME	
DATE PLANTED	
DEPTH PLANTED	
WHEN IN FLOWER	
COMMENTS	

CHECKLIST OF POND TASKS

Spring

Thin out oxygenating plants; remove algae; divide and replant congested plants; carry out new planting; begin feeding fish.

Summer

Remove algae; thin out excessive growth; feed water lilies; feed fish; replenish water lost by evaporation; weed bog garden; take softwood cuttings; collect and sow seed.

Fall

Thin out underwater plants; remove dying growth and debris; net pond to keep out leaves; protect tender plants against cold; stop feeding fish.

Winter

Overhaul pump; ensure small area of surface remains unfrozen by using a heater or a floating ball or log.

DIARY OF POND LIFE

PHOTOGRAPH OF YOUR
WATER GARDEN

SPRING

FALL

SUMMER

WINTER

PART TWO

GARDEN DIARY

Use this section to make monthly notes of what
happens in your garden throughout the year, and to
record visits to gardens, horticultural shows,
and lectures. Detailed checklists will help remind
you of seasonal tasks to be undertaken.

SPRING

The garden bursts into life in spring, heralding the end of winter. The first shoots of bulbs and perennials begin to emerge and leaf buds unfurl on deciduous shrubs. As the earth warms, spring bulbs come into flower. The fresh, delicate green of their new foliage contrasts beautifully with the cheerful hues of their blooms. Pretty pink and white blossoms add a froth of massed color. The air is clear, and the sunshine has a special brightness seen at no other time of the year. Now is the time to start sowing seed, undertake new plantings, and get ahead on routine maintenance to ensure your garden will look its best in the coming year and in the years to come.

Sweet spring, full of sweet days and roses,
A box where sweets compacted lie.
GEORGE HERBERT, *THE TEMPLE*

SPRING GARDEN TASKS

Pruning
Prune deciduous shrubs and climbers that flower on new wood, late summer-flowering trees, and shrubby herbs.

Weeding
Control all weeds.

Mulching
Feed and mulch all established plants, beds, and borders once the soil has warmed up but is still moist.

Spraying
Begin spraying roses, and perennials if necessary, against pests and diseases.

Planting
Plant out trees, shrubs, biennials, pot-grown roses, herbs, and hardy annuals; water new plantings frequently.

Deadheading
Deadhead bulbs and early-flowering plants regularly unless their seed is needed.

Sowing
Sow seeds of hardy perennials and annuals outdoors.

Lawns
Repair damaged areas; sow seed or lay new turf; Begin mowing when grass begins to grow.

Top-dress
Repot or top-dress all plants in containers outdoors and under glass.

General
Prepare greenhouse beds; repair any winter damage to sheds, fences, and paths; clean paths; clean and oil or paint garden furniture.

PHOTOGRAPH OF YOUR GARDEN
IN SPRING

EARLY SPRING

TASKS TO BE DONE

CHECKLIST OF EARLY SPRING TASKS

Clean up winter debris

Plant out hardy perennials and summer-flowering bulbs

Check tree ties and stakes

Layer trees, shrubs, and climbers

Sow seeds of annuals under cover

SPECIAL PROJECTS

PLANTS THAT REQUIRE SPECIAL ATTENTION

IDEAS FOR FUTURE PLANTING

Then came the lovely spring with a rush of blossoms and music,
Flooding the earth with flowers, and the air with melodies vernal.

HENRY LONGFELLOW, *TALES OF A WAYSIDE INN*

THE GARDEN IN EARLY SPRING

PLANTS IN FLOWER

OUTSTANDING PLANTS

SUCCESSFUL COLOR SCHEMES

VERSATILE BULBS

Spring-blooming bulbs provide some of the earliest flowers of the year. Once established, they will increase annually and, with good care, will produce a profusion of flowers for many years. Bulbs extend the flowering season of planting designs before many deciduous shrubs and perennials have emerged from winter hibernation. The wide variety available means that with careful choice you can select bulbs that are suitable for any site and guarantee continuous flowers throughout the year.

After bulbs have finished flowering, remove the blooms, but allow the leaves to die down naturally so that the bulb can build food reserves for the following year. Feed with manure to promote growth for the next flowering season.

WEATHER CONDITIONS

According to folklore, a wedding would occur shortly after bringing honeysuckle into a house. Putting the flower in a girl's bedroom was thought to encourage romantic dreams.

MID-SPRING

TASKS TO BE DONE

SPECIAL PROJECTS

CHECKLIST OF MID-SPRING TASKS

Plant climbers

Introduce biological pest controls into greenhouse

Remove suckers from trees and shrubs

Prune and renovate evergreen shrubs

Reseed or resod worn areas of lawn

Pinch and/or stake herbaceous plants

PLANTS THAT REQUIRE SPECIAL ATTENTION

IDEAS FOR FUTURE PLANTING

The season pricketh every gentle heart,
And maketh him out of his sleep to start.
CHAUCER, *THE KNIGHT'S TALE*

THE GARDEN IN MID-SPRING

PLANTS IN FLOWER

OUTSTANDING PLANTS

SUCCESSFUL COLOR SCHEMES

THE REWARDS OF PRUNING

Pruning is an important way to obtain the optimum performance from a plant, and to encourage it to produce more flowers, fruit, or foliage. It may be done to direct the growth of a young plant into a strong and attractive structure, to train a plant into a particular shape, or to keep a very vigorous plant under control. Weak, diseased, or tired shoots can be removed and the production of flowers and fruit increased. Taking out some old stems also allows light and air into a plant.

The type and time of pruning will depend on the plant – some need little attention, while others grow best when cut back hard. Plants should be fed generously after being cut back, since pruning stimulates new growth.

WEATHER CONDITIONS

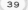

LATE SPRING

TASKS TO BE DONE

CHECKLIST OF LATE SPRING TASKS

Prune early-flowering
shrubs

Start planting out
annuals

Sow biennials
in nursery bed or
under cover

Begin to lift and store
spring-flowering bulbs

Rake lawn and apply
fertilizer

SPECIAL PROJECTS

PLANTS THAT REQUIRE SPECIAL ATTENTION

IDEAS FOR FUTURE PLANTING

The Spring's behaviour here is spent
To make the world magnificent.

JOHN DRINKWATER, *MAY GARDEN*

THE GARDEN IN LATE SPRING

PLANTS IN FLOWER

OUTSTANDING PLANTS

SUCCESSFUL COLOR SCHEMES

THE BENEFITS OF MULCHING

Spring is an ideal time to apply a mulch, because the ground has begun to warm up but remains moist, and weeds have begun to proliferate. A mulch is usually a thick layer of organic matter spread on the soil surface; effective mulches include garden or used mushroom compost, well-rotted manure, shredded hardwood, straw, ground bark, or cocoa shells. Materials such as black plastic or gravel can also be used.

A mulch has a number of advantages: it conserves moisture by reducing evaporation, maintains the ground at an even temperature, keeps plant roots cool, and suppresses weeds. Organic mulches also provide nourishment for plants and improve the water retention, structure, and fertility of the soil. Some organic mulches greatly improve the appearance of a garden, as soil showing between plants can appear thin and bare.

WEATHER CONDITIONS

If the oak's out before the ash, then you'll only get a splash; If the ash precedes the oak, then you may expect a soak.
ENGLISH PROVERB

SUMMER

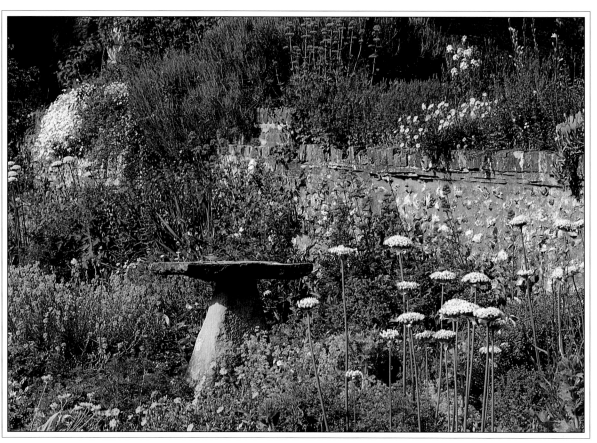

With the intensive work of spring completed, the gardener can begin to slow down and enjoy watching the garden unfold, reaching a full crescendo as summer progresses. The lush summer garden boasts a profusion of flowers and a wealth of rich colors and scents, as the long, hot, days provide optimum conditions for many plants. Routine tasks such as deadheading, spraying, and staking, still need to be carried out regularly so that the carefully planned luxuriance does not become an unruly mess. Summer is ideal for entertaining in the garden, and the gardener should be able to find time to enjoy sharing the fruits of all the labors of spring with friends and family and turn his attention to appreciating the garden he has created.

SUMMER GARDEN TASKS

Pruning
After flowering, prune shrubs and climbers that flower on old wood.

Weeding
Control all weeds.

Staking
Stake late-flowering plants that will need support; check plant ties.

Spraying
Spray plants that are prone to infestation or disease, if desired.

Deadheading
Remove faded flowers regularly unless their seed is needed.

Lawns
Mow frequently, except in dry periods.

Watering
Water containers daily
in dry weather; water newly planted and budding plants thoroughly.

Cutting back
Cut back early-flowering perennials to promote a second flush of growth.

Sowing
Collect and sow seed of early-flowering herbaceous plants and bulbs.

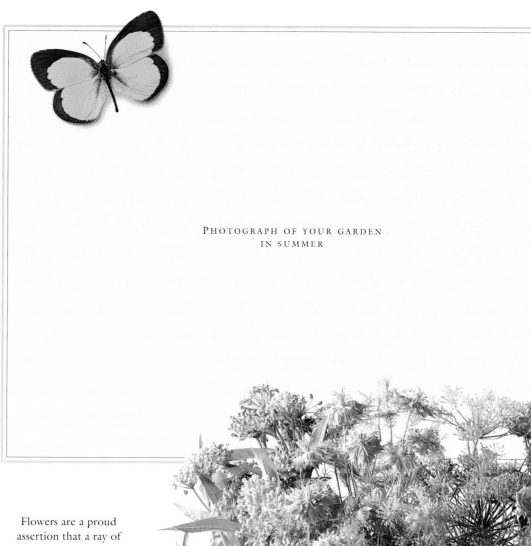

PHOTOGRAPH OF YOUR GARDEN
IN SUMMER

Flowers are a proud assertion that a ray of beauty outvalues all the utilities of the world.

RALPH WALDO EMERSON,
ESSAYS: GIFTS

EARLY SUMMER

....

TASKS TO BE DONE

CHECKLIST OF EARLY
SUMMER TASKS

Shade and ventilate
greenhouse

Lift and store spring-
flowering bulbs

Prune spring-flowering
deciduous trees
and shrubs

Take softwood cuttings
of climbers

Finish planting out
annuals

....

SPECIAL PROJECTS

....

PLANTS THAT REQUIRE SPECIAL ATTENTION

....

IDEAS FOR FUTURE PLANTING

I have a little garden of my own,
But so with roses overgrown,
And Lilies, that you would it guess
To be a little wilderness.

ANDREW MARVELL,
THE NYMPH COMPLAINING OF THE DEATH OF HER FAWN

THE GARDEN IN EARLY SUMMER

PLANTS IN FLOWER

OUTSTANDING PLANTS

STAKING

When fully grown, many modern herbaceous plants collapse under the weight of large, heavy blooms, or their slender stems may be beaten down or broken by wind and rain. Once a plant has flopped over, it is difficult to stake effectively without the supports looking unnatural and obtrusive.

It is best to stake tall or fragile plants early in the growing season – usually spring or early summer – when the foliage is still emerging. This will allow the shoots to grow through the supports into a natural form and new foliage will conceal the staking. Use individual stakes for plants with thick or single stems, and a circle of stakes and twine, or metal link stakes, for clump-forming plants. As the plants grow, remember to tie in plants at intervals to the single stakes or to raise the circular supports slightly.

WEATHER CONDITIONS

SUCCESSFUL COLOR SCHEMES

Midsummer

TASKS TO BE DONE

*CHECKLIST OF
MIDSUMMER TASKS*

Feed roses after
flowering

Begin to plan
fall planting

Prepare soil for
fall planting

Plant fall-flowering
bulbs

Plant out seedlings
of perennials
and biennials into
nursery bed

SPECIAL PROJECTS

PLANTS THAT REQUIRE SPECIAL ATTENTION

IDEAS FOR FUTURE PLANTING

Summer afternoon – Summer
afternoon; to me those have always
been the two most beautiful words
in the English language.
HENRY JAMES, *A BACKWARD GLANCE*

THE GARDEN IN MIDSUMMER

PLANTS IN FLOWER

SUCCESSFUL COLOR SCHEMES

OUTSTANDING PLANTS

WEATHER CONDITIONS

THE VALUE OF WATER

Water is essential to plants and is especially important during the growing season. Prioritize your watering – in a dry spell, newly planted or young plants can rapidly become dehydrated, while larger, more mature plants have established root systems to search for water. Hanging baskets and containers may need watering twice a day in warm weather. Weed thoroughly so that these unwanted plants do not compete for valuable water.

Frequent light watering will evaporate quickly, encourage unwanted root growth near the dry surface, and weaken the plant, so it is best to give a garden plant or border a good, long soaking once a week. Water in the early evening, when the soil can absorb the moisture before it evaporates in the summer sun.

SUMMER BEDDING RECORD

Annuals and tender perennials used as summer bedding plants grow quickly, and provide profuse amounts of colorful flowers for a long period. They are invaluable for brightening areas of the garden that may become drab once spring bulbs and plantings have died down, or where a plant has suddenly died and left a gap. Bedding plants can also be used to fill in spaces while perennial plants are maturing and can be planted in containers for instant color.

They are commonly massed in summer beds for maximum impact, but can add a pleasing random dimension to a mixed border, particularly if they are allowed to self-seed. They offer vibrant color and delightful informality if interspersed throughout the permanent planting of a border – a technique that is especially succesful when much of the garden is not in flower. Annuals, in particular, can add a touch of tropical luxuriance.

BEDDING PLANT	SUPPLIER OR SOURCE	WHERE PLANTED	FLOWERING PERIOD

O, softly on yon banks of haze,
Her rosy face the summer lays.
J. T. TROWBRIDGE, *MIDSUMMER*

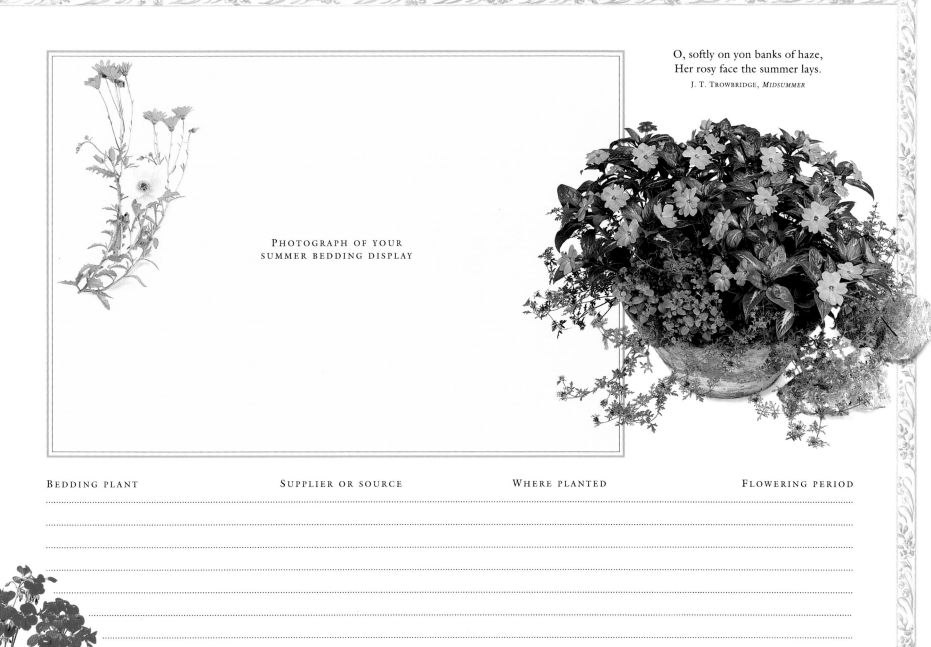

PHOTOGRAPH OF YOUR
SUMMER BEDDING DISPLAY

BEDDING PLANT	SUPPLIER OR SOURCE	WHERE PLANTED	FLOWERING PERIOD

LATE SUMMER

TASKS TO BE DONE

SPECIAL PROJECTS

CHECKLIST OF LATE SUMMER TASKS

Place plant, bulb, and seed orders with nurseries for fall delivery

Take semi-ripe and softwood cuttings of woody plants

Prune topiary, rambler roses, and most old roses

Sow seed of hardy annuals and biennials in pots for fall planting

Start cutting back shrubby herbs

PLANTS THAT REQUIRE SPECIAL ATTENTION

IDEAS FOR FUTURE PLANTING

The purest and most thoughtful minds are those which love colour the most.

JOHN RUSKIN, *THE STONES OF VENICE*

THE GARDEN IN LATE SUMMER

PLANTS IN FLOWER

SUCCESSFUL COLOR SCHEMES

From ancient times, white lilies have represented innocence and purity. Because of this symbolism they often appear in bridal bouquets and wedding arrangements.

OUTSTANDING PLANTS

WEATHER CONDITIONS

CREATIVE COLOR

The summer palette covers the whole spectrum of color and can be as bright or as subtle as you please. Hot colors, such as reds, oranges, and yellows, look their best in the heat and brilliance of the late summer sun. Alternatively, cool colors such as pale pinks, blues, and purples can help to create a welcome feeling of respite; white flowers especially come into their own on a summer's evening, when they seem luminous in the dusk.

Color is one of the crucial elements of any planting design. Hot colors draw the eye and appear nearer, while cool colors are calming and seem more distant. Opposite colors often complement each other; for example, splashes of bold color can add sparkle to a muted color scheme, while pale hues can accentuate a fiery border. Work with related colors in differing intensities as you build confidence in your color choices.

FALL

For man, autumn is
a time of harvest, of
gathering together.
For nature, it is a
time of sowing, of
scattering abroad.

EDWIN WAY TEALE,
AUTUMN ACROSS AMERICA

Fall is a mellow time. The exuberance of summer is over, but there are still some flowers in bloom, and foliage, hips, berries, seedheads, and grasses add rich color and texture to your garden. Sunlight becomes more diffuse and gentle, and it is time for harvest. Visual emphasis moves toward the shape and color of fall foliage and bark. Some plants are at their peak, and with the herbaceous perennials mostly over, fall foliage comes into its own. The shapes and hues of plants and leaves that change color in this season can be used to great effect. Fall shades of red, orange, burgundy, and russet are rich, deep, and warm. One or two carefully placed plants with spectacularly colored leaves, offset by some later-flowering perennials in reds and yellows, will create the perfect seasonal setting for reflection and relaxation.

CHECKLIST OF FALL TASKS

Pruning
Prune deciduous trees, shrubs, and evergreen hedges.

Weeding
Control all weeds.

Mulching
Mulch established plants and borders.

Transplanting
Move established trees, shrubs, and perennials.

Dividing
Divide congested or clump-forming perennials and herbs.

Sowing
Collect and sow seeds of hardy perennials and annuals outside.

Taking cuttings
Take cuttings of tender herbaceous plants; take hardwood cuttings.

Lawns
Reseed worn areas; returf if conditions permit; aerate and apply fall fertilizer; mow and edge as necessary.

Leaves
Collect leaves as they fall, and place in a pile or mesh bin to make compost.

PHOTOGRAPH OF YOUR GARDEN
IN FALL

Planting
Plant out shrubs, climbers, hardy perennials, biennials, pot-grown trees, and spring-flowering bulbs; plant prepared bulbs in pots for forcing.

Winter protection
Pot up tender plants and bring under frost-free cover; protect the crowns of vulnerable plants in the garden; raise and winter-wrap containers.

Cutting back
Cut back dead foliage and remove stakes.

General
Clean out and disinfect the greenhouse; clean outdoor furniture and store; bring in winter-flowering plants under glass and top-dress.

EARLY FALL

TASKS TO BE DONE

CHECKLIST OF EARLY FALL TASKS

Prune evergreen hedges

Plant evergreen hedges

Take semi-ripe and leaf-bud cuttings of trees, shrubs, climbers, and herbs

Take cuttings of tender herbaceous plants

SPECIAL PROJECTS

Sing a song of seasons!
Something bright in all!
Flowers in the summer,
Fires in the fall.

ROBERT LOUIS STEVENSON,
AUTUMN FIRES

PLANTS THAT REQUIRE SPECIAL ATTENTION

IDEAS FOR FUTURE PLANTING

THE GARDEN IN EARLY FALL

PLANTS IN FLOWER

LUSCIOUS LEAF MOLD

Fallen leaves create an exquisite pattern of rich colors on the lawn, but they do need to be raked up and put to good use. Leaves that curl up and resist compaction, such as oak and ash, can help protect plants against frost heaving: cover the crowns of perennials that die down during the winter with a handful of leaves, and secure them with twigs. Leaves can also be left to rot down into leaf mold. Make or buy a wire mesh bin, pack the leaves in loosely, water and turn occasionally, and let them rot down. This creates a crumbly mixture that can be used as a soil conditioner or put through a sieve and added to soil mix.

OUTSTANDING PLANTS

SUCCESSFUL COLOR SCHEMES

*A cherry year
a merry year;
a plum year
a dumb year;
a pear year
a dear year.*
ENGLISH PROVERB

WEATHER CONDITIONS

MID-FALL

TASKS TO BE DONE

CHECKLIST OF MID-FALL TASKS

Plant bare-root and balled-and-burlapped trees

Transplant established shrubs

Plant evergreen shrubs

Carry out layering of shrubs and climbers

Rake out thatch and aerate lawn

Take hardwood cuttings of woody plants

PLANTS THAT REQUIRE SPECIAL ATTENTION

SPECIAL PROJECTS

IDEAS FOR FUTURE PLANTING

Summer ends and Autumn comes, and he who would have it otherwise would have high tide always and a full moon every night.

HAL BORLAND, *SUNDIAL OF THE SEASONS*

THE GARDEN IN MID-FALL

PLANTS IN FLOWER

....

Shelling peas is surrounded by superstitions. It was considered lucky to find a pod containing only a single pea, but even more auspicious to discover one with nine perfect peas.

OUTSTANDING PLANTS

....

SUCCESSFUL COLOR SCHEMES

....

SAVING SEEDS

An easy and inexpensive way of increasing your stock for next year is to collect the seeds from your favorite plants. You can also be certain that the seed is truly fresh. Many hardy annuals and perennials can be sown as soon as the seed has ripened, but it is prudent to keep some back for spring, when the seed can be used for filling in gaps between plants.

Collect the seedheads or pods in paper bags as soon as they begin to ripen or split, and let them dry out completely in a cool, airy place. If the seed is contained in a fleshy fruit or berry, soak the fruit in water to soften the fleshy coating, extract the seed and clean it, then let it dry. Separate out the seed and discard any chaff, put the seeds in labeled envelopes, and store in a cool, dark, dry place until needed.

WEATHER CONDITIONS

LATE FALL

TASKS TO BE DONE

SPECIAL PROJECTS

CHECKLIST OF
LATE FALL TASKS

Take hardwood cuttings
of trees

Sow green manure
on bare soil

Train in new shoots
of climbers

Transplant hardy
perennials and biennials
from nursery bed to
borders

PLANTS THAT REQUIRE SPECIAL ATTENTION

IDEAS FOR FUTURE PLANTING

Season of mists and mellow fruitfulness,
Close bosom friend of the maturing sun;
Conspiring with him how to load and bless
With fruit the vines that round the thatch-eaves run.

JOHN KEATS, *ODE TO AUTUMN*

THE GARDEN IN LATE FALL

PLANTS IN FLOWER

OUTSTANDING PLANTS

SUCCESSFUL COLOR SCHEMES

MAKING COMPOST

Compost-making is a satisfying activity for the gardener, completing the cycle of growth and decay and providing a sumptuously fertile mixture that effectively replenishes soil nutrients. Even the smallest garden can maintain a compost pile.

Any organic matter from the kitchen and garden, laid down in layers of soft and more woody material, will rot down if the pile is kept moist and air is allowed to circulate freely. Bacteria and other organisms such as worms and insects then break up the organic matter to produce heat and the desired crumbly, sweet-smelling mixture. Turning and watering the pile occasionally speeds up decomposition. It is best not to include perennial weeds, meat and fish, or diseased prunings in a compost pile. Compost increases water retention in sandy soil and helps break up heavy clay soil.

WEATHER CONDITIONS

Despite its many uses as a culinary herb, parsley has unlucky associations in folklore. It was believed that it should never be cut by a person in love, transplanted, or given away.

WINTER

The importance of good garden design is revealed in winter, when the garden is stripped down to its bones. Evergreens that provided a constant but unremarkable backdrop to more dynamic plants in the summer can be appreciated without distraction. Attune your eye to the subtle beauty of winter: the delicate shapes created by frost on twigs, leaves, and grasses; the fragile winter sun casting elongated shadows across the lawn; the texture of bark, the color of exposed stems and bright winter berries; and the welcome sight of dainty and exquisite winter flowers. Winter is the year's rest. For maximum impact, position winter-flowering plants with perfumed flowers near the house and enjoy the fragrance from scented winter-flowering plants wafting on the crisp, clear air.

WINTER GARDEN TASKS

Pruning
Prune and renovate deciduous shrubs.

Planting
Plant out trees, shrubs, pot-grown climbers, and roses.

Transplanting
Transplant deciduous trees, young shrubs, and established roses and perennials.

Watering
Water seedlings, cuttings, bulbs, and other plants under glass if needed.

Winter protection
Make sure all plant protection remains secure; check necessary plant ties and supports are in place.

General
Service garden machinery, tools, and water pump; place orders for spring delivery with nurseries and seed companies.

PHOTOGRAPH OF YOUR GARDEN
IN WINTER

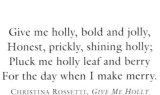

Give me holly, bold and jolly,
Honest, prickly, shining holly;
Pluck me holly leaf and berry
For the day when I make merry.
CHRISTINA ROSSETTI, *GIVE ME HOLLY*

EARLY WINTER

TASKS TO BE DONE

PLANTS THAT REQUIRE SPECIAL ATTENTION

CHECKLIST OF EARLY WINTER TASKS

Prune and renovate deciduous trees and hedges

Take hardwood cuttings of trees, shrubs, and climbers

Finish collecting leaves

Finish clearing away plant debris and stakes

Sow seed of woody plants

SPECIAL PROJECTS

IDEAS FOR FUTURE PLANTING

When nature presents us with barren prospects, there
is something unspeakably cheerful in a spot of
ground which is covered with trees that smile amidst
all the rigours of winter.

JOSEPH ADDISON, *THE SPECTATOR*

THE GARDEN IN EARLY WINTER

PLANTS IN FLOWER OR IN BERRY

SUCCESSFUL COLOR SCHEMES

There are many superstitions attached to the herb rosemary. It was thought that it would only grow for the righteous – and for a woman who was known to rule her husband and her household.

WEATHER CONDITIONS

OUTSTANDING PLANTS

PUTTING THE GARDEN TO BED

As the days shorten and the weather becomes colder, it is time to protect the garden against the cold and winds of winter. Young, delicate plants can be protected with leaf mold, straw, or cloches and windbreaks erected as necessary. Bubble wrap can be tied around containers to be left outside, and the rest brought inside. Erect burlap screens around newly planted evergreens to protect from sun and wind. Gaps that have appeared in the mulch can be filled in, to prevent the frost from penetrating too deeply into the soil. Take advantage of the bareness of the garden and carry out general maintenance of tools, fences, and paths, or undertake structural work such as digging a pond or building a rock garden or gazebo.

MID-AND LATE WINTER

TASKS TO BE DONE

CHECKLIST OF MID- AND LATE WINTER TASKS

Repot or top-dress trees in containers

Prepare trees for layering in spring

Prune and train hardy deciduous climbers

Graft trees and shrubs

Brush snow from shrubs and hedges

Repair storm damage

SPECIAL PROJECTS

PLANTS THAT REQUIRE SPECIAL ATTENTION

IDEAS FOR FUTURE PLANTING

It is a winter's tale
That the snow blind twilight ferries over the lakes
And floating fields from the farm in the cup of the vales.

DYLAN THOMAS, *A WINTER'S TALE*

THE GARDEN IN MID- AND LATE WINTER

PLANTS IN FLOWER OR IN BERRY

ADVANCE PLANNING

The depths of winter, when there is less to do in the garden, is an ideal time to take stock and plan for the coming year. The notes you have made during the previous seasons will prove invaluable in helping you choose which plants and seeds to buy in order to improve your garden in the following year. Now is the time to plan a whole new area and decide to try out new ideas – to incorporate plants previously unknown to you into existing planting, or to experiment with planting combinations that you have noticed and admired during the previous year.

OUTSTANDING PLANTS

SUCCESSFUL COLOR SCHEMES

*Holly has been seen as a symbol of eternal life for centuries and is widely thought to be a lucky plant.
A holly hedge around a house was believed to keep out evil influences.*

WEATHER CONDITIONS

GARDENS VISITED

Visiting other gardens, whether they are historically famous, interesting, or simply beautiful to look at, is a wonderful way to learn the art of gardening. You can get new ideas and expand the breadth of your knowledge. Seeing an unfamiliar plant growing is an effortless way to become aware of new plants, and noticing a planting combination that you find particularly appealing will give you inspiration for new plants and ideas for your own garden. Making notes soon after a visit will help you remember remarkable gardens.

NAME OF GARDEN

ADDRESS

DATE OF VISIT

OUTSTANDING PLANTS

NOTES

NAME OF GARDEN

ADDRESS

DATE OF VISIT

OUTSTANDING PLANTS

NOTES

NAME OF GARDEN

ADDRESS

DATE OF VISIT

OUTSTANDING PLANTS

NOTES

NAME OF GARDEN

ADDRESS

DATE OF VISIT

OUTSTANDING PLANTS

NOTES

NAME OF GARDEN

ADDRESS

DATE OF VISIT

OUTSTANDING PLANTS

NOTES

NAME OF GARDEN

ADDRESS

DATE OF VISIT

OUTSTANDING PLANTS

NOTES

NAME OF GARDEN

ADDRESS

DATE OF VISIT

OUTSTANDING PLANTS

NOTES

PHOTOGRAPH OR
MEMENTO OF VISIT

NAME OF GARDEN

ADDRESS

DATE OF VISIT

OUTSTANDING PLANTS

NOTES

SHOWS AND LECTURES

An enthusiastic gardener is aware that there will always be a great deal to learn and many new plants and ideas to discover. Visiting flower shows and attending lectures or taking courses are enjoyable ways to augment your gardening knowledge. At flower shows you can find out about current trends in gardening and discover which new plants are being introduced, while a comprehensive lecture or course can give a lot of information – and be entertaining. Use these pages to make notes of everything you wish to remember or use in your plans for the future.

FLOWER SHOWS

NAME OF SHOW
....

DATE OF VISIT
....

OUTSTANDING PLANTS

....

NEW PLANTS SEEN

....

NEW IDEAS

....

NEW NURSERIES AND SUPPLIERS

....

COMMENTS

_____

NAME OF SHOW
....

DATE OF VISIT
....

OUTSTANDING PLANTS

....

NEW PLANTS SEEN

....

NEW IDEAS

....

NEW NURSERIES AND SUPPLIERS

....

COMMENTS

_____

LECTURES

NAME OF SPEAKER ....

PLACE/DATE ....

TOPIC OF TALK ....

COMMENTS ....

NAME OF SPEAKER ....

PLACE/DATE ....

TOPIC OF TALK ....

COMMENTS ....

NAME OF SHOW ....

DATE OF VISIT ....

OUTSTANDING PLANTS ....

NAME OF SPEAKER ....

PLACE/DATE ....

TOPIC OF TALK ....

COMMENTS ....

NEW PLANTS SEEN ....

NAME OF SPEAKER ....

PLACE/DATE ....

TOPIC OF TALK ....

NEW IDEAS ....

COMMENTS ....

NEW NURSERIES AND SUPPLIERS ....

NAME OF SPEAKER ....

PLACE/DATE ....

TOPIC OF TALK ....

COMMENTS ....

COMMENTS ....

CONTACT NAMES AND ADDRESSES

Use this section to record the details of the nurseries, suppliers, and individuals
you use for all your gardening requirements.

NAME

ADDRESS

TELEPHONE/CONTACT NAME

COMMENTS

NAME

ADDRESS

TELEPHONE/CONTACT NAME

COMMENTS

NAME

ADDRESS

TELEPHONE

CONTACT NAME

COMMENTS

NAME

ADDRESS

TELEPHONE/CONTACT NAME

COMMENTS

NAME

ADDRESS

TELEPHONE/CONTACT NAME

COMMENTS

NAME

ADDRESS

TELEPHONE

CONTACT NAME

COMMENTS

NAME

ADDRESS

NAME

ADDRESS

TELEPHONE/CONTACT NAME

COMMENTS

TELEPHONE/CONTACT NAME

COMMENTS

NAME

ADDRESS

NAME

ADDRESS

TELEPHONE/CONTACT NAME

COMMENTS

TELEPHONE/CONTACT NAME

COMMENTS

NAME

ADDRESS

NAME

ADDRESS

TELEPHONE

CONTACT NAME

COMMENTS

TELEPHONE

CONTACT NAME

COMMENTS

Membership Records

NATIONAL HOME
GARDENING CLUB

Use this page to record your membership details of horticultural organizations.

ORGANIZATION

MEMBERSHIP NUMBER

SUBSCRIPTION

DATE DUE

NOTES

ORGANIZATION

MEMBERSHIP NUMBER

SUBSCRIPTION

DATE DUE

NOTES

ORGANIZATION

MEMBERSHIP NUMBER

SUBSCRIPTION

DATE DUE

NOTES

ORGANIZATION

MEMBERSHIP NUMBER

SUBSCRIPTION

DATE DUE

NOTES

ACKNOWLEDGMENTS

Dorling Kindersley would like to thank the following for their
kind assistance in supplying items for special photography:
Castle Antiques, Lewes; Kennedy's Garden Centre, Hailsham;
McQueens, London.

The following photographs were reproduced by courtesy of:
Jerry Harpur, pages 4 and 60; Anne Hyde, page 34;
S. & O. Mathews, page 42.